Animal Lives

THE LIFE OF A DOG

By Jan Feder
Illustrated by Tilman Michalski

CHILDRENS PRESS INTERNATIONAL
CHICAGO

Library of Congress Cataloging in Publication Data

Feder, Jan.
  The life of a dog.

  (Animal lives)
  Translation of: Der Hund.
  Summary: An account of a year in the life of a farm
watchdog, followed by text and illustrations presenting
the physical characteristics, behavior, and history of
dogs.
  1. Dogs—Juvenile literature. [1. Dogs.
2. Dogs—Fiction] I. Michalski, Tilman, ill.
II. Title. III. Series.
SF426.5.F413 1982   636.7   82-9752
ISBN 0-516-08932-3

North American 1982 Edition published
by Regensteiner Publishing Enterprises, Inc.

Bella was barking. She always barked when a strange person or animal came into the farmyard. It was her job to guard the farm. This time it was only a friend coming to visit the farmer's wife.

Bella was very loyal to the farmer and his family. She had adopted them as her own family. Since there was no dog pack for her to live with, Bella obeyed the farmer and his family as she would have obeyed the leaders of a pack.

The farm was her territory, and she watched over it well.

Bella knew all the people and animals who belonged on the farm. She knew them by their scent. Dogs have a very keen sense of smell.

The animals knew Bella, too. They knew that they had nothing to fear from her, though the farmyard cat usually kept out of her way.

Suddenly Bella caught an unfamiliar smell. There was a stranger in the farmyard. Bella picked up the trail at once. She ran along following it, with her nose close to the ground.

The stranger dashed across the farmyard. The chickens scattered in alarm.

It was a cat. Attracted by the smell of fresh milk, the cat had come into the farmyard. The cat could hear Bella's panting breath behind it. Bella was getting closer and closer. The cat was in danger now. It looked desperately for a safe place.

With a daring leap the cat jumped onto the farmyard wall. Now it was safe. It turned to face Bella, arching its back and hissing. Bella barked and barked. Finally the cat jumped down on the other side of the wall and left.

Bella was pleased with herself. She had driven the cat away.
At the same time she was restless. She felt the urge to go wandering. In fact she was ready to mate. Bella went looking for a male dog.

She had not been out long when she met Boy. He lived on the next farm. Boy usually avoided Bella. She could be very fierce at times. But today she was different. She ran to meet Boy. The two dogs sniffed each other. Bella licked Boy on the nose.

Boy was surprised. Suddenly Bella ran away. Startled, Boy chased her. It was some time before he could catch up with her. When he did, they mated.

A little while later the two dogs parted. Bella made her way back to her own farmyard.

Nine weeks later Bella gave birth to a litter of four puppies. She had made herself a nest in the hay in the stable. The puppies were born there. For the first week or more they were blind.

At first Bella would not let anyone near her puppies, not even the farmer. But later she brought them into the farmhouse. She even let the children pick them up.

After a couple of months the farmer found good homes for the puppies. One dog was enough on the farm.

The year went by. The days became shorter. It got dark quite early in the afternoon. Soon winter came—a cold, hard winter—the worst for years. Bella would have liked to stay in the warm farmhouse. But she had to guard the farm. She had to sleep out in her kennel at night.

The deep snow made it hard for wild animals to find food. Even the timid rabbits came into the farmyard at night to eat bark off the trees and bushes.

And one wild, dangerous creature—the fox—crept closer and closer to the farmyard.

Finally one night, the fox came into the farmyard. He tried to get into the hen house. The noise the hens made woke Bella. She came charging up, barking and barking.

The fox tried to slip past Bella, but she blocked his way. He snapped at her and made his escape.

By this time the farmer had come out. He was just in time to see the fox disappearing into the darkness.

"Good girl, Bella," said the farmer. "He won't come back in a hurry." He checked to make sure Bella was not hurt. Then he went back to bed.

In fact, as a reward for driving away the fox, Bella got a large, meaty bone.

Bella was a good guard dog. She kept the farm and the family safe. In return the farmer fed her and cared for her.

The Domestic Dog

A descendant of the wolf

Animals that hunt and eat other animals are called beasts of prey. The scientific name for them is Carnivora. The canine (dog) family, or Canidae, belong to the Carnivora. The wolf is the biggest and strongest member of the family, which also includes the jackal, the coyote, the fox, and the domestic dog. As far as we can tell, the dog is probably descended from wolves. It is easy to see this relationship if you are looking at a German Shepherd, but harder to see if you look at a dachshund or a toy poodle. We can compare the physical structure of members of the canine family, their skulls and teeth, and particularly their behavior. Everything points to a close relationship between wolves and dogs. We have to say "wolves" and not "wolf," because there were, and still are, many different wolves in different parts of the world. There is the European, or Northern, wolf, the Indian wolf, and the Chinese wolf. Each is different.

The different species of wolf would not mate together in their wild state. But when humans tamed wolves and brought them to live with them, deliberate breeding began. The result was many different breeds of dog. Of course, the process took tens of thousands of years. Today, we know of about 400 different breeds of dog. The American Kennel Club lists 125 kinds.

How dogs came to live with people

The first domesticated animals were wolves. They are the ancestors of our domestic dogs. Perhaps hunters in prehistoric times caught and tamed small wolves. Or perhaps wolves followed the nomadic hunters, or came close to their caves or mud huts to eat remains of food that had been thrown away. Wolves will feed on carrion as well as killing and eating living prey. So they act as scavengers. Wolves normally live and hunt in organized groups, or packs. They adapted quite easily to living with groups of people.

It may have been just by chance that people now began mating different kinds of domesticated wolves. But it may be that they realized they could breed to bring out characteristics that would be useful. They could raise faster hounds for hunting or more watchful ones for guard dogs. The ancient Egyptians, for instance, needed hounds that would run very fast to hunt the swift animals of the plains. So they bred dogs like greyhounds.

The training of dogs

The longer the domestic dog (or Canis familiaris, to give it its scientific Latin name) lived with people, the more it was trained to be useful. In time it turned out that some breeds were better than others for particular work. So people purposely bred dogs that would be suitable for special jobs. They needed dogs of various kinds for hunting. They needed swift dogs with good staying power, like Afghans, for running

down prey. Sturdy, short-legged dogs, like dachshunds, were used to drive animals out of their burrows. Hounds with a very good sense of smell, like foxhounds, followed game. Today, we know which dogs can do which tasks if they are brought up to do so. That means that the dog must be trained, and even take examinations. A gundog, for instance, must learn to stay at heel, whether on or off the leash. He must keep quiet at the sound of a shot, and find and retrieve a dead creature.

Besides hounds for hunting, and sheepdogs, we now have dogs specially trained to help people in disasters. There are avalanche rescue dogs that can find people buried under masses of snow (German Shepherds, Airedale terriers, Rottweilers, and St. Bernards are particularly suitable). Dogs can be trained to search mines, or act as ambulance dogs. There are guide dogs for the blind (German Shepherds, Labradors, boxers, and Rottweilers are probably the best). Recently, dogs have been trained to help deaf or partially deaf people, by making them aware of certain noises such as the ringing of an alarm or a baby's crying. Police dogs have been

Dogs who Work with Man

Hound (pointer)

Sheepdog (red kelpie)

Police dog

Avalanche rescue dog (St Bernard)

Guidedog
(Labrador)

Sled dog
(husky)

used for some time to track down criminals. Now there are some dogs especially trained to sniff out drugs. The sled dogs of the Eskimos (Greenland dogs and huskies) have even given rise to a new sport, dog-sled racing. A good dog team can reach a top speed of up to 25 miles (40 kilometers) an hour.

The dog's senses

There are over four hundred different breeds of dog. Not much can be said that will apply to every single one of them. But physical structure, the shape of skull and jaws, and most of all the dog's senses, show that all dogs are beasts of prey.

As a hunter, the dog needs good senses of smell, sight, and hearing. In fact, a dog's sense of smell is far keener than that of other animals. A dog can pick up a scent after only a moment or so sniffing around. Then he can follow the trail for many miles. The dog's sense of smell is so good, at least in the various breeds of dog used as hounds, that probably only the wolf has a better one.

The dog also has a very good sense of hearing. It hears the slightest sound that we ourselves can catch, and can also pick up high notes beyond the range of the human ear. However, its sense of sight is not quite so good. In fact, many breeds of dog have quite weak eyesight. In old age the dog's vision gets worse. Eye diseases are very common in dogs. However, the way the eyes are placed means that the dog can see better than many other animals. Dogs are thought to be color-blind.

Dogs and their young

A young female can have puppies herself at the age of six to eight months. Females are ready to mate twice a year. They attract male dogs by the special smell of their urine. A female may happen to mate with two males at this time. Then puppies of different kinds, with different fathers, can appear in the same litter. Pregnancy lasts 63 days on the average. The number of puppies in the litter varies.

The puppies stay in the nest and are blind at first. But their sense of

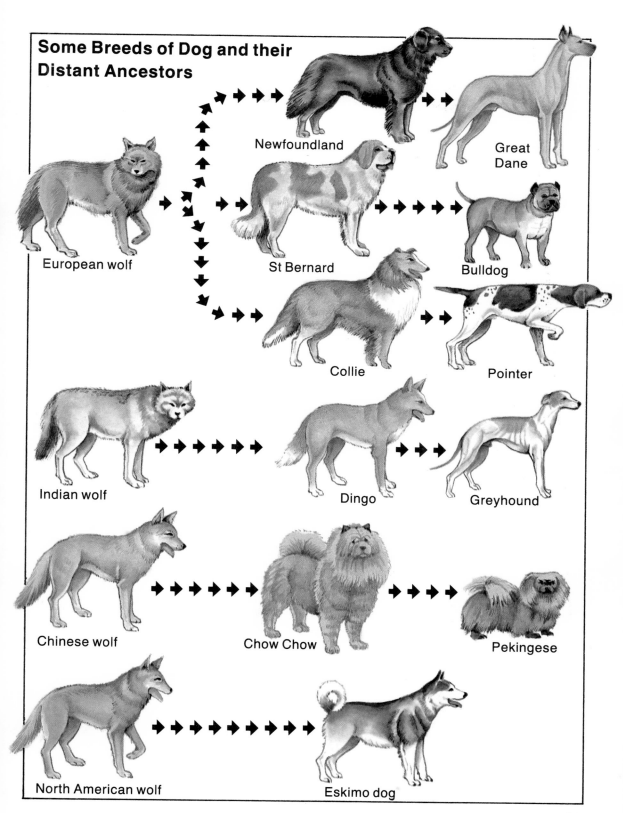

Some Breeds of Dog and their Distant Ancestors

Newfoundland

Great Dane

European wolf

St Bernard

Bulldog

Collie

Pointer

Indian wolf

Dingo

Greyhound

Chinese wolf

Chow Chow

Pekingese

North American wolf

Eskimo dog

Some Breeds of Dog

Alsatian
(German Shepherd)

German spaniel

Small
Münsterländer

Smooth
dachshund

Afghan hound

Standard
poodle

Cocker spaniel

Boxer

Standard
schnauzer

Dalmatian

Collie

Wire-haired
fox terrier

smell is well developed. They can find their way to their mother's teats. She suckles them for four weeks, and sometimes for two or three weeks longer. But after the first four weeks their main food is meat. The puppies open their eyes after eight to ten days, but it is at least another three months before their sight is fully developed. To begin with, puppies crawl rather than walk. They start walking properly when they are about ten days old. At the age of one month they can follow their mother.

Puppies should not be taken away from their mothers too early. For the first 8 or 9 weeks they are learning important lessons in their games with their brothers and sisters. They learn how to approach another dog, for example, and all the signs described on pages 28-29.

The father, if he is around, is usually very even tempered with the puppies.

Meeting and fighting

Like wolves, who live in packs, dogs are sociable animals. Domestic dogs cannot usually live in packs themselves. So they adopt their masters or the families they belong to as "pack leaders."

If treated properly by humans, the dog recognizes its place in the ranking order (the order of seniority) and will be obedient. If a dog is disobedient, he may well be trying to move up in the ranking order by challenging someone above him, as he would do in a pack.

The dog is a member of a community. It will defend its own territory, whether it is a farmyard or house. It marks this territory out with its urine (it can be trained not to do this in the house). A town dog will include its daily walks in its territory. It may come to regard a public park as its own property. It will try to cover up new scent marks left by other dogs with its own urine. And if it does meet a strange dog in its territory, it will immediately show who is master. A well-trained dog will not actually attack the intruder. But it will growl in an unmistakable way. The growling enables it to keep its self-respect.

When it comes to a dogfight, dogs do not always rush at each other straight away. Their behavior varies from breed to breed and dog to dog. For instance, if two dogs are equally strong, they will try to alarm one another, taking up a position intended to be impressive. They

Special Breeds of Dog

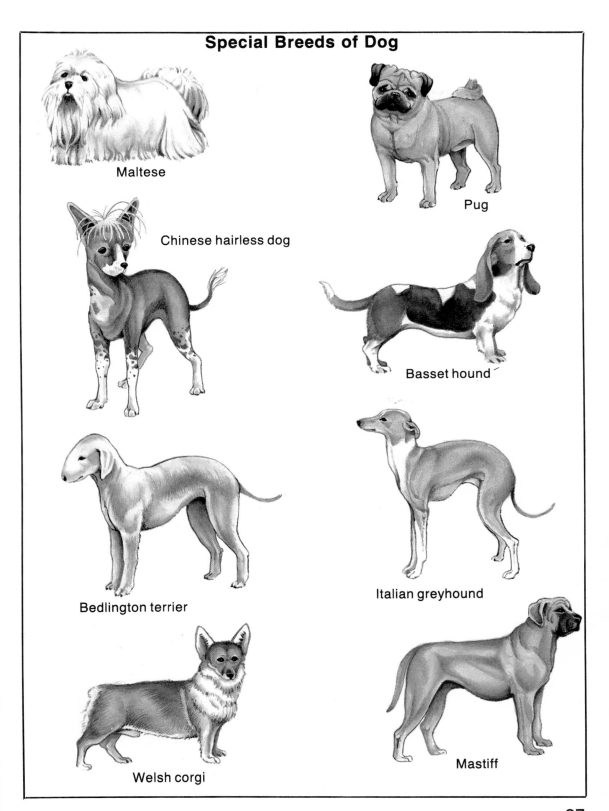

Maltese

Pug

Chinese hairless dog

Basset hound

Bedlington terrier

Italian greyhound

Welsh corgi

Mastiff

bare their teeth and prick up their ears, their coats bristle so they look bigger. They raise their tails and stand at a sideways angle to each other, glaring. If neither will give in to the threats of the other, a real fight usually follows. First the two dogs run at each other, each trying to fling its opponent to the ground. Then each may attack the muzzle, ears, and throat of its opponent. If a dog is admitting defeat, it lies on its back with its throat exposed. This means total surrender. The fight is over. The defeated dog usually slinks away with its tail between its legs.

The language of the dog

A dog's bark is not its only means of communication. You can tell, from its barking, whether a dog wants to give you a warning or welcome you happily. A growling noise means that the dog is ready to attack. A howl means pain. A whine means the dog is begging or asking for something. However, the dog's face and tail and the way it holds its body give us clearer information about what it is trying to say—look at the illustrations on page 29.

A dog holds its head high and pricks up its ears to show that it is interested and paying attention. Its tail may be either raised or relaxed and hanging down. If the dog wants to welcome someone, it wags its tail and usually raises one paw. If it is asking for a game, it generally crouches playfully in front of you, wagging its tail hard.

A dog is threatening to attack when it stretches its head forward, lays back its ears, and bares its teeth. Its tail is either coiled or raised straight upwards. The hair on its back and the nape of its neck bristles. The dog is showing fear when it lowers its head, lays back its ears, and puts its tail between its back legs. Sometimes it goes down on all fours at the same time, to express submission.

When a dog shows a human being the whites of its eyes (which makes it look very guilty), it is saying that it recognizes that particular human as its master. Dog communicates with dog in the same way.

The Language of the Dog

Language of the face:

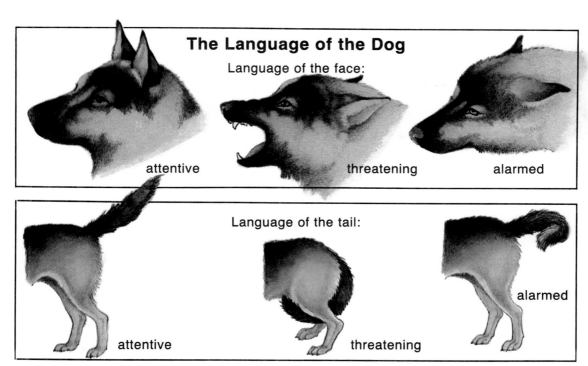

attentive

threatening

alarmed

Language of the tail:

attentive

threatening

alarmed

Language of the body:

attentive

threatening

asking
for a game

relaxed

submissive

alarmed

Interesting Facts about the Dog

The earliest representations of dogs
The oldest pictorial representations we have of dogs come to us from the Babylonians, Egyptians, and Chinese. They showed hounds or watchdogs in pictures, reliefs, and small statues. For instance, the "lion dogs" of the emperors of China, which looked like large, fierce Pekingese, guarded the palaces and are shown in statues as household guardians.

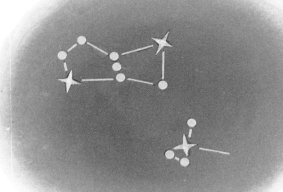

The Great Dog and the Little Dog
The Great Dog and the Little Dog are two constellations of stars. The ancient Greeks believed that the two hounds went hunting with the huntsman Orion, who also gave his name to a constellation. The Hare, another constellation, crouches at Orion's feet. The brightest star in the Great Dog is Sirius; in fact, it is the brightest of all the fixed stars. It is known as the Dog Star. The ancient Egyptians calculated their calendar year from this star. There is another constellation called the Hunting Dogs.

The fighting dogs of the Romans
We are told that the Romans used dogs in war. These dogs even wore iron armor during battle. The dog collar is also thought to have been invented by the Romans. At first it was an iron ring set with sharp spikes, to protect the dog from bites in a fight. Later dog collars were used as ornaments to show off the wealth of the dog's owners.

Dogs in our language
There are a lot of phrases referring to dogs, perhaps because dogs have lived with humans for so long. For example, "a dog's life" is a miserable life. If someone makes "a dog's dinner" of something, he makes it very untidy. To be "dog tired" is to be quite worn out. A "dog-eared" book has the pages bent down at the corners like a dog's ear. A "dog's tooth" check is a broken-check pattern often used in the weaving of tweed. A "dog leg" in a flight of stairs is where it turns a corner, making an angle like a dog's hind leg, with some tapering steps like those in a spiral staircase.

Canine records
The heaviest dog is the St. Bernard. A fully

grown St. Bernard often weighs more than 250 pounds (113 kilos). The record is 287 pounds (130 kilos). The tallest dog is the Irish wolfhound, which stands over a yard (meter) tall at the shoulder. The smallest and one of the lightest dogs is the Mexican chihuahua, which stands only 6 inches (15 centimeters) tall at the shoulder, and usually weighs less than a pound (half a kilo). The fastest dog is the borzoi, which reaches an average speed of 37 miles (60

kilometers) an hour. The rarest dog is probably the Sha-pei or Russian war dog. There are thought to be only fifteen such dogs in the world. The dog's record for long jumping is 30 feet (9 meters), held by a greyhound. The record for high jumping is about 11 feet (3.5 meters), held by a German Shepherd.

Dogfights
Fights arranged between dogs and other dogs, or dogs and bulls or bears, were regarded as entertainment for centuries. They were popular in the Middle Ages. Cruel fights of this kind were not made illegal until the nineteenth century in some countries.

Famous dogs in literature
The Greek poet Homer tells us, in the *Odyssey,* that the hero Odysseus had a dog called Argos. When Odysseus came home after wandering for twenty years, Argos was the first to recognize him, but the old dog immediately died of joy. The poet Elizabeth Barrett Browning owned a spaniel called Flush, and wrote a poem to him. Later on the writer Virginia Woolf wrote a biography of Flush. The famous poet Lord Byron wrote an epitaph for the grave of his Newfoundland dog Boatswain.

Some odd facts
A dog cannot sweat to cool itself down. Instead it opens its mouth, sticks out its tongue, and pants. As the moisture evaporates, it draws heat from the dog's body.

The basset hound can describe circles with the tip of its tail, which no other dog can do. The red kelpie, an Australian sheepdog, guides its flock of sheep by running along the backs of the crowd of animals and barking.

The prairie dog is not a dog at all, or even a carnivorous animal, but a rodent. It gets its name because it makes a barking sound like a dog.

Lapdogs
Lapdogs were fashionable as long ago as the Middle Ages. One theory is that people believed the dogs would attract any fleas to themselves, so keeping human beings free of them. Another is that they acted as live hot-water bottles.

From beauty parlor to cemetery
Poodles were originally clipped because it was thought they could swim more easily if their hind legs were shaved. They were used to retrieve game from the water. Later on, however, poodle clipping became simply a matter of fashion.

There are beauty parlors, and even special restaurants, for dogs. In America, there are large cemeteries for dogs, where people's pets are buried as if they were human beings. The graves are often marked not by simple gravestones, but by expensive, elaborate buildings like little temples.

Index